Women Daily Q by Inspiring Women

Compiled by

Georgiana Carollus

ISBN-13: 978-0615629131

DEDICATION

To Mary Ann, Skip, and Dennis – words fail me when I try to express my gratitude for your love and support.
Thank you for all you did to help bring this book to life!

ACKNOWLEDGEMENTS

With gratitude and appreciation to the women whose inspiring words are compiled in this book. And, a special shout-out to Wikipedia for providing an invaluable resource for author information.

CONTENTS

INTRODUCTION

I have always loved quotations and it has been a pleasure to compile this collection of inspiring words by women. While there are hundreds of quotation books published, women's words are usually vastly outnumbered by those of men. I enjoyed researching thousands of quotes to find these nuggets of wit and wisdom.

I have assigned a different topic to each month and collected quotations that relate to that topic. You can use this book for daily inspiration or review the quotes on a specific topic when you need a fresh perspective.

However you use this book, I hope you have an experience I often have with quotes – as if by magic, the quote I read is just what I need at that moment!

Enjoy!

Georgiana Carollus

JANUARY: CHANGE

1

Change is the constant, the signal for rebirth,

the egg of the phoenix.

Christina Baldwin, in One to One (1977)

JANUARY: CHANGE

2

With the only certainty in our daily existence

being change, and a rate of change

growing always faster in a kind of

technological leapfrog game,

speed helps people think they are keeping up.

Gail Sheehy, American social critic and writer, 1936-

JANUARY: CHANGE

3

Living in the past is a dull and lonely business;

looking back strains the neck muscles,

causes you to bump into people

not going your way.

Edna Ferber, American playwright and novelist, 1887-1968

JANUARY: CHANGE

4

I realized that if what we call

human nature can be changed,

then absolutely anything is possible.

And, from that moment, my life changed.

Shirley MacLaine, American actor, activist, and writer, 1934-

JANUARY: CHANGE

5

If you don't like something, change it.

If you can't change it, change your attitude.

Don't complain.

Maya Angelou, American poet, activist, storyteller, and actor, 1928-

JANUARY: CHANGE

6

I have not ceased being fearful,

but I have ceased to let fear control me.

I have accepted fear as a part of life –

specifically the fear of change,

the fear of the unknown,

and I have gone ahead despite

the pounding in my heart that says:

turn back, turn back,

you'll die if you venture too far.

Erica Jong, American poet and writer, 1942-

JANUARY: CHANGE

7

Those interested in perpetuating

present conditions are always in tears

about the marvelous past

that is about to disappear,

without having so much as

a smile for the young future.

Simone De Beauvoir, The Second Sex (1949)

JANUARY: CHANGE

8

The moment of change is the only poem.

Adrienne Rich, American poet, essayist, and feminist, 1929-2012

JANUARY: CHANGE

9

To keep our faces toward change and

behave like free spirits

in the presence of fate

is strength undefeatable.

Helen Keller, American lecturer and writer, first deaf blind person to earn a Bachelor of Arts degree, 1880-1968

JANUARY: CHANGE

10

Nothing is so painful to the human mind

as a great and sudden change.

Mary Wollstonecraft Shelley, English novelist and short story writer, 1797-1851

JANUARY: CHANGE

11

Although the connections are

not always obvious,

personal change is inseparable

from social and political change.

Harriet Lerner, Dance of Intimacy (1989)

JANUARY: CHANGE

12

Growth itself contains the germ of happiness.

Pearl S. Buck, American writer, 1892-1973

JANUARY: CHANGE

13

The only thing that makes life possible is

permanent, intolerable uncertainty:

not knowing what comes next.

Ursula K. LeGuin, American author, Nebula and Hugo Awards winner, 1929-

JANUARY: CHANGE

14

People change and forget to tell one another.

Lillian Hellman, American author of plays and memoirs, 1905-1984

JANUARY: CHANGE

15

If one is going to change things,

one has to make a fuss

and catch the eye of the world.

Elizabeth Janeway, American author and critic, 1913-2005

JANUARY: CHANGE

16

We live in an epoch in which the solid ground

of our preconceived ideas

shakes daily under our certain feet.

Barbara Ward, British economist and writer, 1914-1981

JANUARY: CHANGE

17

But people themselves alter so much,

that there is something new

to be observed in them for ever.

Jane Austen, English novelist, 1775-1817

JANUARY: CHANGE

18

All adventures,

especially into new territory,

are scary.

Sally Ride, American astronaut, first American woman in space, 1951-

JANUARY: CHANGE

19

The need for change

bulldozed a road

down the center of my mind.

Maya Angelou, American poet, activist, storyteller, and actor, 1928-

JANUARY: CHANGE

20

Changes are not only possible and predictable,

but to deny them is to be

an accomplice to one's

own unnecessary vegetation.

Gail Sheehy, American social critic and writer, 1936-

JANUARY: CHANGE

21

You gain strength, courage,

and confidence by every experience

in which you really stop

to look fear in the face.

You must do the thing which

you think you cannot do.

Eleanor Roosevelt, American humanitarian and First Lady, 1884-1962

JANUARY: CHANGE

22

It is wonderful how quickly

you get used to things,

even the most astonishing.

Edith Nesbit, English writer and poet, 1858-1924

JANUARY: CHANGE

23

None of us knows what the

next change is going to be,

what unexpected opportunity is

just around the corner,

waiting to change all the tenor of our lives.

Kathleen Norris, American novelist, 1880-1966

JANUARY: CHANGE

24

Time is a dressmaker specializing in alterations.

Faith Baldwin, American writer, 1893-1978

JANUARY: CHANGE

25

There is no sin punished

more implacably by nature

than the sin of resistance to change.

Anne Morrow Lindbergh, American nonfiction writer and poet, 1906-2001

JANUARY: CHANGE

26

Everything in life that we really accept

undergoes a change.

Katherine Mansfield, prominent modernist writer of short fiction, 1888-1923

JANUARY: CHANGE

27

If we don't change, we don't grow.

If we don't grow, we are not really living.

Growth demands a

temporary surrender of security.

Gail Sheehy, American social critic and writer, 1936-

JANUARY: CHANGE

28

The tragedy of life is that people do not change.

Agatha Christie, British crime writer, 1890-1976

JANUARY: CHANGE

29

Some things . . . arrive in their

own mysterious hour,

on their own terms and not yours,

to be seized or relinquished forever.

Gail Godwin, American novelist and short story writer, 1937-

JANUARY: CHANGE

30

Never doubt that a small group of

thoughtful, committed citizens

can change the world.

Indeed, it's the only thing that ever has.

Margaret Mead, American cultural anthropologist, 1901-1978

31

Continuity gives us roots;

change gives us branches,

letting us stretch and grow

and reach new heights.

Pauline R. Kezer, American politician

FEBRUARY: DREAMS AND AMBITIONS

1

You can have anything you want if

you want it desperately enough.

You must want it with an inner exuberance

that erupts through the skin and

joins the energy that created the world.

Sheilah Graham, American nationally syndicated gossip columnist, 1904-1988

FEBRUARY: DREAMS AND AMBITIONS

2

Don't be afraid of the space

between your dreams and reality.

If you can dream it, you can make it so.

Belva Davis, broadcast journalist

FEBRUARY: DREAMS AND AMBITIONS

3

In each of us are places

where we have never gone.

Only by pressing the limits

do you ever find them.

Dr. Joyce Brothers, American psychologist, TV personality, and advice columnist, 1927-

FEBRUARY: DREAMS AND AMBITIONS

4

There are many ways of breaking a heart.

Stories were full of hearts broken by love,

but what really broke a heart

was taking away its dream –

whatever that dream might be.

Pearl S. Buck, American writer, 1892-1973

FEBRUARY: DREAMS AND AMBITIONS

5

There are people who put their dreams
in a little box, and say, "Yes, I've got dreams,
of course, I've got dreams." Then they put the box
away and bring it out once in awhile to look in it,
and yep, they're still there. These are *great* dreams,
but they never get out of the box.
It takes an uncommon amount of guts
to put your dreams on the line, to hold them up,
and say, "How good or how bad am I?"
That's where courage comes in.

Erma Bombeck, American humorist, 1927-1996

FEBRUARY: DREAMS AND AMBITIONS

6

Without leaps of imagination, or dreaming,

we lose the excitement of possibilities.

Dreaming, after all, is a form of planning.

Gloria Steinem, American feminist, journalist, social and political activist, 1934-

FEBRUARY: DREAMS AND AMBITIONS

7

Imagination is the highest kite one can fly.

Lauren Bacall, American film and stage actor, 1924-

FEBRUARY: DREAMS AND AMBITIONS

8

We all have our own life to pursue,

our own kind of dream to be weaving.

And we all have some power

to make wishes come true,

as long as we keep believing.

Louisa May Alcott, American novelist,
1832-1888

FEBRUARY: DREAMS AND AMBITIONS

9

Stop the habit of wishful thinking and

start the habit of thoughtful wishes.

Mary Martin, American actress, 1913-1990

FEBRUARY: DREAMS AND AMBITIONS

10

Dreams are like paper, they tear so easily.

Gilda Radner, American comedian and performer, 1946-1989

FEBRUARY: DREAMS AND AMBITIONS

11

The future belongs to those who believe

in the beauty of their dreams.

Eleanor Roosevelt, American humanitarian and First Lady, 1884-1962

FEBRUARY: DREAMS AND AMBITIONS

12

Reach high, for stars lie hidden in your soul.

Dream deep, for every dream

precedes the goal.

Pamela Vaull Starr, poet and writer, 1909-1993

FEBRUARY: DREAMS AND AMBITIONS

13

The dream was always running ahead of one.

To catch up, to live for a moment

in unison with it,

that was the miracle.

Anaïs Nin, French-Cuban author, 1903-1977

FEBRUARY: DREAMS AND AMBITIONS

14

Rose-colored glasses are

never made in bifocals.

Nobody wants to read the

small print in dreams.

Ann Landers (Esther Pauline Friedman),
advice columnist, 1918-2002

FEBRUARY: DREAMS AND AMBITIONS

15

Were there none who were discontented

with what they have,

the world would never reach anything better.

Florence Nightingale, celebrated English nurse and writer, 1820-1910

FEBRUARY: DREAMS AND AMBITIONS

16

Our faith in the present dies out

long before our faith in the future.

Ruth Benedict, American anthropologist and folklorist, 1887-1948

FEBRUARY: DREAMS AND AMBITIONS

17

Only when men are connected to large,

universal goals are they are really happy –

and one result of their happiness

is a rush of creative activity.

Joyce Carol Oates, American writer, 1938-

FEBRUARY: DREAMS AND AMBITIONS

18

Dreams are, by definition,

cursed with short life spans.

Candice Bergen, American actor and screenwriter, 1946-

FEBRUARY: DREAMS AND AMBITIONS

19

Throw your dreams into space like a kite,

and you do not know what it will bring back:

a new life, a new friend,

a new love, a new country.

Anaïs Nin, French-Cuban author, 1903-1977

FEBRUARY: DREAMS AND AMBITIONS

20

I've dreamt in my life dreams
that have stayed with me ever since
and changed my ideas:
they've gone through and through me,
like wine through water,
and altered the color of my mind.

Emily Bronte, British novelist and poet, 1818-1848

FEBRUARY: DREAMS AND AMBITIONS

21

When people keep telling you that

you can't do a thing,

you kind of like to try it.

Margaret Chase Smith,
announcing her presidential candidacy, 1964

FEBRUARY: DREAMS AND AMBITIONS

22

Is there anything better than

to be longing for something,

when you know it is within reach?

Greta Garbo, Swedish-American actor, 1905-1990

FEBRUARY: DREAMS AND AMBITIONS

23

We cast away priceless time in dreams,

born of imagination, fed upon illusion,

and put to death by reality.

Judy Garland, American singer and stage actor,
1922-1969

FEBRUARY: DREAMS AND AMBITIONS

24

Cut not the wings of your dreams,

for they are the heartbeat

and the freedom of your soul.

Flavia, English literary critic and poet, 1661-1720

FEBRUARY: DREAMS AND AMBITIONS

25

If one is lucky, a solitary fantasy

can totally transform one million realities.

Maya Angelou, American poet, activist, storyteller, and actor, 1928-

FEBRUARY: DREAMS AND AMBITIONS

26

Dreams pass into the reality of action.

From the actions stems the dream again;

and this interdependence produces

the highest form of living.

Anaïs Nin, French-Cuban author, 1903-1977

FEBRUARY: DREAMS AND AMBITIONS

27

Our deepest wishes are

whispers of our authentic selves.

We must learn to respect them.

We must learn to listen.

Sarah Ban Breathnach, author of
Simple Abundance

FEBRUARY: DREAMS AND AMBITIONS

28

To anyone who has a dream,

I say follow that dream.

You are never too old.

It is never too late.

Susan Boyle, Scottish singer, 1961-

FEBRUARY: DREAMS AND AMBITIONS

29

If growing up is the process of

creating ideas and dreams

about what life should be,

then maturity is letting go again.

Mary Beth Danielson, American columnist

MARCH: JOY

1

Joy is what happens to us

when we allow ourselves to recognize

how good things really are.

Marianne Williamson, American spiritual activist, author, and founder of The Peace Alliance, 1953-

MARCH: JOY

2

What is joy?

A sunbeam between two clouds.

Madame Deluzy, French actress, 1747-1830

MARCH: JOY

3

We could never learn to be brave and patient,

if there were only joy in the world.

Helen Keller, American lecturer and writer, first deaf blind person to earn a Bachelor of Arts degree, 1880-1968

MARCH: JOY

4

There are random moments - tossing a salad,
coming up the driveway to the house,
ironing the seams flat on a quilt square,
standing at the kitchen window and
looking out at the delphiniums,
hearing a burst of laughter
from one of my children's rooms –
when I feel a wavelike rush of joy.
This is my true religion: arbitrary moments of
nearly painful happiness for a life
I feel privileged to lead.

Elizabeth Berg, American novelist, 1948-

MARCH: JOY

5

If you celebrate your differentness,

the world will, too.

It believes exactly what you tell it—

through the words you use to describe yourself,

the actions you take to care for yourself,

and the choices you make to express yourself.

Tell the world you are one-of-a-kind creation

who came here to experience

wonder and spread joy.

Expect to be accommodated.

Victoria Moran, American writer on spirituality and nutrition topics

MARCH: JOY

6

When we experience moments of ecstasy -

in play, in art, in sex – they come not as an

exception, an accident, but as a taste of what life is

meant to be. . . Ecstasy is an idea, a goal, but it can

be the expectation of every day. Those times when

we're grounded in our body, pure in our heart,

clear in our mind, rooted in our soul, and suffused

with the energy, the spirit of life, are our birthright.

It's a natural human gift

that should be at the heart of our lives.

Gabrielle Roth, American musician, 1941-

MARCH: JOY

7

I define joy as a sustained sense

of well-being and internal peace –

a connection to what matters.

Oprah Winfrey, American producer and actor, 1954-

MARCH: JOY

8

Learning to live in the present moment

is part of the path of joy.

Sarah Ban Breathnach, author of
Simple Abundance

MARCH: JOY

9

Beauty is whatever gives joy.

Edna St. Vincent Millay, American lyrical poet and feminist, 1882-1950

MARCH: JOY

10

If we can just let go and trust that things

will work out they way they're supposed to,

without trying to control the outcome,

then we can begin to enjoy

the moment more fully.

The joy of the freedom it brings becomes

more pleasurable than the experience itself.

Goldie Hawn, American actor, film producer, and director, 1945-

MARCH: JOY

11

To be happy--one must find one's bliss.

Gloria Vanderbilt, American artist, author, and socialite, 1924-

MARCH: JOY

12

People from a planet without flowers

would think we must be mad with joy

the whole time to have such things about us.

Iris Murdoch, Irish-born British author and philosopher, 1919-1999

MARCH: JOY

13

In my own worst seasons I've come back from the
colorless world of despair by forcing myself to look
hard, for a long time, at a single glorious thing:
a flame of red geranium outside my bedroom
window. And then another: my daughter in a yellow
dress. And another: the perfect outline of a
full, dark sphere behind the crescent moon.
Until I learned to be in love with my life again.
Like a stroke victim retraining
new parts of the brain to grasp lost skills,
I have taught myself joy, over and over again.

Barbara Kingsolver, American novelist, 1955-

MARCH: JOY

14

Find ecstasy in life;

the mere sense of living is joy enough.

Emily Dickinson, American poet, 1830-1886

MARCH: JOY

15

An infinite question is often

destroyed by finite answers.

To define everything is to annihilate much

that gives us laughter and joy.

Madeleine L'Engle, American young adult fiction author, 1918-2007

MARCH: JOY

16

Join the great company of those who make the barren places of life fruitful with kindness. Carry a vision of heaven in your hearts. Your success and happiness lie within you. External conditions are the accidents of life, its outer wrappings. The great, enduring realities are love and service. Joy is the holy fire that keeps our purpose warm and our intelligence aglow. Resolve to keep happy, and your joy and you shall form an invincible host against difficulty.

Helen Keller, American lecturer and writer, 1880-1968

MARCH: JOY

17

Joy must be one of the pivots of our life.

It is the token of a generous personality.

Sometimes it is also a mantle

that clothes a life of sacrifice and self-giving.

A person who has this gift

often reaches high summits.

He or she is like sun in a community.

Mother Teresa, humanitarian and
Nobel Peace Prize recipient, 1910-1997

MARCH: JOY

18

Joy seems to me a step beyond happiness –

happiness is a sort of atmosphere

you can live in sometimes

when you're lucky.

Joy is a light that fills you with

hope and faith and love.

Adela Rogers St. Johns, American journalist and novelist, 1894-1988

MARCH: JOY

19

It was strange, I reflected...

that even in the weirdest circumstances,

the most troubling episodes of one's life,

the greatest divides from

home and familiarity,

there were these moments

of undeniable joy.

Elizabeth Kostova, American novelist, 1964-

MARCH: JOY

20

Joy is the soul made visible.

Susan Santucci, Pathways to the Spirit, 1999

MARCH: JOY

21

The excursion is the same

when you go looking for your sorrow

as when you go looking for your joy.

Eudora Welty, American author, 1909-2001

MARCH: JOY

22

People need joy as much as clothing.

Some of them need it far more.

Margaret Collier Graham, American writer, 1850-1910

MARCH: JOY

23

And for a moment - for a split second -

everything else falls away,

the whole pattern and order of my life,

and a huge joy crests in my chest.

I am no one, and I owe nothing to anybody,

and my life is my own.

Lauren Oliver, American author

MARCH: JOY

24

Joy is the characteristic by which God

uses us to re-make the

distressing into the desired,

the discarded into the creative.

Joy is prayer - Joy is strength - Joy is love -

Joy is a net of love by which

you can catch souls.

Mother Teresa, humanitarian and
Nobel Peace Prize recipient, 1910-1997

MARCH: JOY

25

There is no joy involved in

following others' expectations of yourself.

Miriam Toews, Swing Low

MARCH: JOY

26

I like joy; I want to be joyous.

I want to smile and I want

to make people laugh.

And that's all I want.

I like being happy.

I want to make others happy.

Doris Day, American actor and animal rights activist, 1924-

MARCH: JOY

27

If you are joyful,

do not worry about lukewarmness.

Joy will shine in your eyes and in your look,

in your conversation

and in your countenance.

You will not be able to hide it

because joy overflows.

Mother Teresa, humanitarian and
Nobel Peace Prize recipient, 1910-1997

MARCH: JOY

28

May we all soon go about as our real selves

and take joy in it, saying,

yes, yes, to whatever we are.

Carol Emshwiller, American writer of avant garde short stories, 1921-

MARCH: JOY

29

Embrace fanaticism.

Harness joie de vivre by pursuing insane interests, consuming passions, and constant sources of gratification that do not depend on the approval of others.

Elizabeth Wurtzel, American attorney, writer, and journalist, 1967-

MARCH: JOY

30

Joy seems to me a step beyond happiness—

happiness is a sort of atmosphere

you can live in

sometimes when you're lucky.

Joy is a light that fills you with

hope and faith and love.

Adela Rogers St. Johns, American journalist, novelist, and screenwriter, 1894-1988

MARCH: JOY

31

I found more joy in sorrow

Than you could find in joy.

Sara Teasdale, American lyrical poet, 1884-1933

APRIL: LOVE AND FRIENDSHIP

1

Love is a force. It is not a result; it is a cause.

It is not a product; it produces.

It is a power, like money or steam or electricity.

Anne Morrow Lindbergh, American nonfiction writer and poet, 1906-2001

APRIL: LOVE AND FRIENDSHIP

1

Love is a great beautifier.

Louisa May Alcott, American novelist, 1832-1888

APRIL: LOVE AND FRIENDSHIP

3

Love doesn't just sit there like a stone;

it has to be made, like bread;

remade all the time, made new.

Ursula K. LeGuin, American author,
Nebula and Hugo Awards winner, 1929-

APRIL: LOVE AND FRIENDSHIP

4

The sweetest joy, the wildest woe is love.

Pearl Bailey, American actor and singer, 1916-1990

APRIL: LOVE AND FRIENDSHIP

5

We love because it's the only true adventure.

Nikki Giovanni, American poet and activist, 1943-

APRIL: LOVE AND FRIENDSHIP

6

Love, like truth,

is the unassailable defense.

Diane Ackerman, American author, poet, and naturalist, 1948-

APRIL: LOVE AND FRIENDSHIP

7

Love is the extremely difficult realization

that something other than oneself is real.

Iris Murdoch, Irish-born British author and philosopher, 1919-1999

APRIL: LOVE AND FRIENDSHIP

8

We are not held back by the love

we didn't receive in the past,

but by the love we're not extending in the present.

Marianne Williamson, American spiritual activist, author, and founder of The Peace Alliance, 1953-

APRIL: LOVE AND FRIENDSHIP

9

What we have once enjoyed we can never lose.

All that we deeply love becomes a part of us.

Helen Keller, American lecturer and writer, first deaf blind person to earn a Bachelor of Arts degree, 1880-1968

APRIL: LOVE AND FRIENDSHIP

10

There is no magician like love.

Marguerite Blessington, Irish novelist, 1789-1849

APRIL: LOVE AND FRIENDSHIP

11

The easiest kind of relationship for me

is with ten thousand people.

The hardest is with one.

Joan Baez, American folk singer, 1941-

APRIL: LOVE AND FRIENDSHIP

12

I wonder why love is so often equated

with joy when it is everything else as well.

Devastation, balm, obsession,

granting and receiving excessive value,

and losing it again.

It is recognition, often of

what you are not but might be.

It sears and it heals.

It is beyond pity and above law.

It can seem like truth.

Florida Scott-Maxwell. American playwright and author, 1883-1979

APRIL: LOVE AND FRIENDSHIP

13

There is no mistaking love.

You feel it in your heart.

It is the common fiber of life,

the flame that heats our soul,

energizes our spirit,

and supplies passion to our lives.

Elisabeth Kubler Ross, Swiss American psychiatrist, author, and pioneer in Near-death studies, 1926-2004

APRIL: LOVE AND FRIENDSHIP

14

I have found the paradox,

that if you love until it hurts,

there can be no more hurt,

only more love.

Mother Teresa, humanitarian and
Nobel Peace Prize recipient, 1910-1997

APRIL: LOVE AND FRIENDSHIP

15

To love is to receive a glimpse of heaven.

Karen Sunde, American playwright and screenwriter, 1942-

APRIL: LOVE AND FRIENDSHIP

16

Every time we love,

every time we give,

it's Christmas.

Dale Evans, American writer, film star, and singer, 1912-2001

APRIL: LOVE AND FRIENDSHIP

17

Age does not protect you from love.

But love, to some extent,

protects you from age.

Jeanne Moreau, French actress, singer, screenwriter, and director, 1928-

APRIL: LOVE AND FRIENDSHIP

18

We can only learn to love by loving.

Iris Murdoch, Irish-born British author and philosopher, 1919-1999

APRIL: LOVE AND FRIENDSHIP

19

Each friend represents a world in us,

a world possibly not born until they arrive,

and it is only by this meeting

that a new world is born.

Anaïs Nin, French-Cuban author, 1903-1977

APRIL: LOVE AND FRIENDSHIP

20

I truly feel that there are as many ways of loving as
there are people in the world and as
there are days in the life of those people.

Mary S. Calderone, public health advocate for sex education, 1904-1998

APRIL: LOVE AND FRIENDSHIP

21

Love is a wonderful thing.

You never have to take it away

From one person to give it to another.

There's always more than enough to go around.

Pamela de Roy

APRIL: LOVE AND FRIENDSHIP

22

Love and the hope of it

are not things one can learn;

they are part of life's heritage.

Maria Montessori, Italian educator, 1870-1952

APRIL: LOVE AND FRIENDSHIP

23

Love is the wild card of existence.

Rita Mae Brown, American writer and feminist, 1944-

APRIL: LOVE AND FRIENDSHIP

24

Love is a force

more formidable than any other.

It is invisible - it cannot be seen or measured -

yet it is powerful enough to

transform you in a moment,

and offer you more than

any material possession ever could.

Barbara De Angelis, American relationship consultant and author, 1951-

APRIL: LOVE AND FRIENDSHIP

25

The best proof of love is trust.

Joyce Brothers, American psychologist and advice columnist, 1927-

APRIL: LOVE AND FRIENDSHIP

26

Love is a fruit in season at all times,

and within the reach of every hand.

Mother Teresa, humanitarian and
Nobel Peace Prize recipient, 1910-1997

APRIL: LOVE AND FRIENDSHIP

27

Falling in love consists merely in uncorking the imagination and bottling the common-sense.

Helen Rowland, American journalist and humorist, 1875-1950

APRIL: LOVE AND FRIENDSHIP

28

I Love, and the world is mine.

Florence Earle Coates, American poet, 1850-1927

APRIL: LOVE AND FRIENDSHIP

29

Love's greatest gift is its

ability to make everything it touches sacred.

Barbara De Angelis, American relationship consultant and author, 1951-

APRIL: LOVE AND FRIENDSHIP

30

Whoever has loved knows all

that life contains of sorrow and of joy.

George Sand (Amantine Dupin), French novelist and memoirist, 1804-1876

MAY: SELF-LOVE

1

I believe that when all the dreams are dead

you're left only with yourself.

You'd better like yourself a lot.

Rita Mae Brown, American writer and feminist, 1944-

MAY: SELF-LOVE

2

Seek not outside yourself;

heaven is within.

Mary Lou Cook

MAY: SELF-LOVE

3

You can be pleased with nothing

when you are not pleased with yourself.

Lady Mary Wortley Montagu, English writer, 1689-1762

MAY: SELF-LOVE

4

To say something nice about themselves,

this is the hardest thing in the world

for people to do.

They'd rather take their clothes off.

Nancy Friday, writer on topics of female sexuality and liberation, 1933-

MAY: SELF-LOVE

5

"Ah! if only there were two of me," she thought,

"one who spoke and the other who listened,

one who lived and the other who watched,

how I would love myself!

I'd envy no one."

Simone de Beauvoir, French existentialist philosopher and political activist, 1908-1986

MAY: SELF-LOVE

6

I don't like myself,

I'm crazy about myself.

*Mae West, American actor and playwright,
1893-1980*

MAY: SELF-LOVE

7

I've finally stopped running away from myself.

Who else is there better to be?

Goldie Hawn, American actor, film producer, and director, 1945-

MAY: SELF-LOVE

8

Love yourself first and

everything else falls into line.

You really have to love yourself

to get anything done in this world.

Lucille Ball, American comedian, film and TV star, 1911-1989

MAY: SELF-LOVE

9

I must undertake to love myself

and to respect myself as though

my very life depends upon

self-love and self-respect.

Maya Angelou, American poet, activist, storyteller, and actor, 1928-

MAY: SELF-LOVE

10

It is hard to fight an enemy

who has outposts

in your head.

Sally Kempton, American writer and feminist, 1943-

MAY: SELF-LOVE

11

You need to claim the events of your life

to make yourself yours.

When you truly possess

all you have been and done,

which may take some time,

you are fierce with reality.

Florida Scott-Maxwell. American playwright and author, 1883-1979

MAY: SELF-LOVE

12

When you recover or discover something

that nourishes your soul and bring joy,

care enough about yourself

to make room for it in your life.

Jean Shinoda Bolen, psychiatrist and author, 1936-

MAY: SELF-LOVE

13

Let the world know you as you are,

not as you think you should be,

because sooner or later,

if you are posing, you will forget the pose,

and then where are you?

Fanny Brice, American singer and comedian, 1891-1951

MAY: SELF-LOVE

14

The worst walls are never

the ones you find in your way.

The worst walls are the ones you put there –

you build yourself.

Those are the high ones, the thick ones,

the ones with no doors in.

Ursula K. LeGuin, American author,
Nebula and Hugo Awards winner, 1929-

MAY: SELF-LOVE

15

Love is the great miracle cure.

Loving ourselves works miracles in our lives.

Louise L. Hay, American motivational author, 1926-

MAY: SELF-LOVE

16

The ultimate lesson all of us have to learn

is unconditional love,

which includes not only others

but ourselves as well

Elisabeth Kubler Ross, Swiss American psychiatrist, author, and pioneer in Near-death studies, 1926-2004

MAY: SELF-LOVE

17

Let me listen to me

and not to them.

Gertrude Stein, American writer and playwright, 1874-1946

MAY: SELF-LOVE

18

You cannot belong to anyone else,

until you belong to yourself.

Pearl Bailey, American singer and writer, 1918-1986

MAY: SELF-LOVE

19

I am the only real truth I know.

Jean Rhys, West Indian/English novelist, 1890-1979

MAY: SELF-LOVE

20

If we really love ourselves,

everything in our life works.

Louise L. Hay, American motivational author, 1926-

MAY: SELF-LOVE

21

Love your self's self

where it lives.

Anne Sexton, American poet, 1928-1974

MAY: SELF-LOVE

22

Self-esteem isn't everything;

it's just that there's nothing without it.

Gloria Steinem, American feminist, journalist, and social and political activist, 1934-

MAY: SELF-LOVE

23

Oh, I'm so inadequate!

And I love myself!

Meg Ryan, American actor and producer, 1961-

MAY: SELF-LOVE

24

Did your mom ever tell you,

'If you can't say something nice,

don't say anything'?

She was right -

and talking nicely also applies

when you're talking to yourself,

even inside your head.

Victoria Moran, American writer on spirituality and nutrition topics

MAY: SELF-LOVE

25

May you have the strength to

enjoy your weaknesses.

Florence Edwards

MAY: SELF-LOVE

26

When we begin to take our failures nonseriously,

it means we are ceasing to be afraid of them.

It is of immense importance

to learn to laugh at ourselves.

Katherine Mansfield, New Zealand-born modernist writer of short fiction, 1888-1923

MAY: SELF-LOVE

27

I don't need a man to rectify my existence.

The most profound relationship

we'll ever have is the one with ourselves.

Shirley MacLaine, American actor, activist, and writer, 1934-

MAY: SELF-LOVE

28

Don't compromise yourself.

You are all you've got.

Janis Joplin, American singer and songwriter, 1943-1970

MAY: SELF-LOVE

29

If you aren't good at loving yourself,

you will have a difficult time loving anyone,

since you'll resent the time and energy

you give another person

that you aren't even giving to yourself.

Barbara De Angelis, American relationship consultant and author, 1951-

MAY: SELF-LOVE

30

I was raised to sense

what someone wanted me to be

and be that kind of person.

It took me a long time

not to judge myself

through someone else's eyes.

Sally Field, American actor, producer, director, and screenwriter, 1946-

MAY: SELF-LOVE

31

When a woman becomes her own best friend

life is easier.

Diane Von Furstenberg, Belgian-American fashion designer, 1946-

JUNE: SUCCESS

1

Success doesn't come to you.

You go to it.

Marva Collins, American educator, 1936-

JUNE: SUCCESS

2

The road to success is

always under construction.

Lily Tomlin, American actor, comedian, writer, and producer, 1939-

JUNE: SUCCESS

3

Life is a succession of moments.

To live each one is to succeed.

Corita Kent, artist and educator, 1918-1986

JUNE: SUCCESS

4

Winning the (Nobel) prize wasn't

half as exciting as doing the work itself.

Maria Goeppert Mayer, German-born American theoretical physicist and Nobel laureate in Physics, 1906-1972

JUNE: SUCCESS

5

Success breeds confidence.

Beryl Markham, British-born Kenyan aviatrix and adventurer, 1902-1986

JUNE: SUCCESS

6

You may be disappointed if you fail,

but you are doomed if you don't try.

Beverly Sills, American operatic soprano, 1929-2007

JUNE: SUCCESS

7

To follow, without halt, one aim:

There's the secret of success.

Anna Pavlova, one of the finest classical ballet dancers in history, 1881-1931

JUNE: SUCCESS

8

For you to be successful,

sacrifices must be made.

It's better that they are made by others

but failing that,

you'll have to make them yourself.

Rita Mae Brown, American writer and feminist, 1944-

JUNE: SUCCESS

9

People fall forward to success.

Mary Kay Ash, founder of Mary Kay Cosmetics, 1918-2001

JUNE: SUCCESS

10

Apparent failure may hold in its rough shell

the germs of a success that

will blossom in time,

and bear fruit throughout eternity.

Frances Ellen Watkins Harper, African-American abolitionist, poet and author, 1825-1911

JUNE: SUCCESS

11

I must admit that I personally measure success in terms of the contributions an individual makes to her or his fellow human beings.

Margaret Mead, American cultural anthropologist, 1901-1978

JUNE: SUCCESS

12

Some of the biggest failures

I ever had were successes.

Pearl S. Buck, American writer, 1892-1973

JUNE: SUCCESS

13

We must not, in trying to think

about how we can make a big difference,

ignore the small daily differences we can make

which, over time, add up to

big differences that we often cannot foresee.

Marian Wright Edelman, American activist for children's rights, 1939-

JUNE: SUCCESS

14

I don't confuse greatness with perfection.

To be great anyhow is . . .

the higher achievement.

Lois McMaster Bujold, American author of science fiction, 1949-

JUNE: SUCCESS

15

Success can make you go one of two ways.

It can make you a prima donna –

or it can smooth the edges,

take away the insecurities,

and let the nice things come out.

Barbara Walters, American broadcast journalist, author, and television personality, 1929-

JUNE: SUCCESS

16

I've grown to realize the joy that comes from

little victories is preferable

to the fun that comes from

ease and the pursuit of pleasure.

Lawana Blackwell, The Courtship of the Vicar's Daughter, 1998

JUNE: SUCCESS

17

She's the kind of woman who climbed

the ladder of success – wrong by wrong.

Mae West, American actor and playwright, 1893-1980

JUNE: SUCCESS

18

My personal recipe for success is:

Do what you love and don't look at the clock.

Ann Landers, pen name for advice columnist, Esther Lederer, 1918-2002

JUNE: SUCCESS

19

If you can react the

same way to winning and losing,

that's a big accomplishment.

That quality is important because

it stays with you the rest of your life,

and there's going to be a life after tennis

that's a lot longer than your tennis life.

Chris Evert Lloyd, former world
#1 professional tennis player, 1954-

JUNE: SUCCESS

20

Winning may not be everything,

but losing has little to recommend it.

Dianne Feinstein, senior US Senator from California, 1933-

JUNE: SUCCESS

21

Act as if it were impossible to fail.

Dorothea Brande, American writer and editor, 1893-1948

JUNE: SUCCESS

22

I have made it a rule of my life

never to regret and never to look back.

Regret is an appalling waste of energy...

you can't build on it;

it's only good for wallowing in.

Katherine Mansfield, New Zealand-born modernist writer of short fiction, 1888-1923

JUNE: SUCCESS

23

It had long since come to my attention that people of accomplishment rarely sat back and let things happen to them.

They went out and happened to things.

Elinor Smith, world's youngest licensed pilot at age 16, 1911-2010

JUNE: SUCCESS

24

Failure is impossible.

Susan B. Anthony, prominent American civil rights leader, 1820-1906

JUNE: SUCCESS

25

This became a credo of mine:

attempt the impossible in order

to improve your work.

Bette Davis, American actor of film, television, and theater, 1908-1989

JUNE: SUCCESS

26

You can stand tall

without standing on someone.

You can be a victor

without having victims.

Harriet Woods, American politician and activist, 1927-2007

JUNE: SUCCESS

27

Will and energy sometimes prove greater

than either genius or talent or temperament.

Isadora Duncan, inventor of the American modern dance, 1877-1927

JUNE: SUCCESS

28

What material success does is

provide you with the ability to

concentrate on other things that really matter.

And that is being able to make a difference,

not only in your own life,

but in other people's lives.

Oprah Winfrey, American producer
and actor, 1954-

JUNE: SUCCESS

29

Integrity is perishable

in the summer months of success.

Vanessa Redgrave, political activist and English actor of stage, screen, and television, 1937-

JUNE: SUCCESS

30

Success will win you

false friends and true enemies—

succeed anyway.

Mother Teresa, humanitarian and
Nobel Peace Prize recipient, 1910-1997

JULY: FACING THE FUTURE

1

No one from the beginning of time

has had security.

Eleanor Roosevelt, American humanitarian and First Lady, 1884-1962

JULY: FACING THE FUTURE

2

Hope is the thing with feathers

That perches in the soul.

And sings the tune

Without the words,

and never stops at all.

Emily Dickinson, American poet, 1830-1886

JULY: FACING THE FUTURE

3

The very least you can do in your life

is to figure out what you hope for.

And the most you can do

is live inside that hope.

Barbara Kingsolver, American novelist and poet, 1955-

JULY: FACING THE FUTURE

4

The optimism of a healthy mind

is indefatigable.

Margery Allingham, English crime writer, 1904-1965

JULY: FACING THE FUTURE

5

Truly nothing is to be expected

but the unexpected.

Alice James, American diarist, 1848-1892

JULY: FACING THE FUTURE

6

Faith and doubt are both needed –

not as antagonists but working side by side –

to take us around the unknown curve.

Lillian Smith, American wrier
and social critic, 1897-1966

JULY: FACING THE FUTURE

7

You live with your thoughts –

so be careful what they are.

Eva Arrington

JULY: FACING THE FUTURE

8

Love recognizes no barriers.

It jumps hurdles, leaps fences, penetrates walls

to arrive at it destination full of hope.

Maya Angelou, American poet, activist, storyteller, and actor, 1928-

JULY: FACING THE FUTURE

9

One of the things I learned the hard way

was that it doesn't pay to get discouraged.

Keeping busy and making optimism a way of life

can restore your faith in yourself.

Lucille Ball, American comedian, film and TV star, 1911-1989

JULY: FACING THE FUTURE

10

Hope is a very unruly emotion.

Gloria Steinem, American feminist, journalist, and social and political activist, 1934-

JULY: FACING THE FUTURE

11

To eat bread without hope

is still slowly to starve to death.

Pearl S. Buck, American writer, 1892-1973

JULY: FACING THE FUTURE

12

After all, tomorrow is another day.

Margaret Mitchell, Gone with the Wind, 1900-1949

JULY: FACING THE FUTURE

13

Faith is an excitement and an enthusiasm,

a state of intellectual magnificence

which we must not squander

on our way through life.

George Sand (Amantine Dupin), French novelist and memoirist, 1804-1876

JULY: FACING THE FUTURE

14

Optimism is the faith that leads to achievement.

Nothing can be done without hope and confidence.

Helen Keller, American lecturer and writer, first deaf blind person to earn a Bachelor of Arts degree, 1880-1968

JULY: FACING THE FUTURE

15

It's a long old road,

but I know I'm gonna find the end.

Bessie Smith, American blues singer, 1894-1937

JULY: FACING THE FUTURE

16

Light tomorrow with today.

Elizabeth Barrett Browning, English Victorian-era poet, 1806-1861

JULY: FACING THE FUTURE

17

But what we call our despair is often

only the painful eagerness of unfed hope.

George Eliot (Mary Ann Evans), English novelist and journalist, 1819-1880

JULY: FACING THE FUTURE

18

Every thought we think is creating our future.

Louise L. Hay, American motivational author, 1926-

JULY: FACING THE FUTURE

19

Where will I be five years from now?

I delight in not knowing.

Marlo Thomas, American performer, producer, and social activist, 1937-

JULY: FACING THE FUTURE

20

Never grow a wishbone, daughter,

where a backbone ought to be.

Clementine Paddleford, American food writer, 1898-1967

JULY: FACING THE FUTURE

21

To keep a lamp burning,

we have to keep putting oil in it.

Mother Teresa, humanitarian and
Nobel Peace Prize recipient, 1910-1997

JULY: FACING THE FUTURE

22

Not Truth, but Faith

it is that keeps the world alive.

Edna St. Vincent Millay, American lyrical poet, and feminist, 1882-1950

JULY: FACING THE FUTURE

23

You may not always have a comfortable life
and you will not always be able
to solve all of the world's problems at once
but don't ever underestimate
the importance you can have
because history has shown us that
courage can be contagious and
hope can take on a life of its own.

Michelle Obama, attorney and First Lady, 1964-

JULY: FACING THE FUTURE

24

No great deed is done

by falterers who ask for certainty.

George Eliot (Mary Ann Evans), English novelist and journalist, 1819-1880

JULY: FACING THE FUTURE

25

Hope begins in the dark,

the stubborn hope that if you just show up

and try to do the right thing,

the dawn will come.

You wait and watch and work:

you don't give up.

Anne Lamott, American novelist and non-fiction writer, 1954-

JULY: FACING THE FUTURE

26

What is destructive is impatience, haste,

expecting too much too fast.

May Sarton, American poet, novelist, and memoirist, 1912-1995

JULY: FACING THE FUTURE

27

We grow in time to trust

the future for our answers.

Ruth Benedict, American anthropologist and folklorist, 1887-1948

JULY: FACING THE FUTURE

28

Hope is a renewable option:

If you run out of it at the end of the day,

you get to start over in the morning.

Barbara Kingsolver, American novelist and poet, 1955-

JULY: FACING THE FUTURE

29

You need to get up in the morning and say,

"Boy, I'm going to – in my own stupid way –

save the world today."

Carol Bellamy, social activist, 1942-

JULY: FACING THE FUTURE

30

Love the moment,

and the energy of that moment

will spread beyond all boundaries.

Corita Kent, artist and educator, 1918-1986

JULY: FACING THE FUTURE

31

And the trouble is,

if you don't risk anything,

you risk even more.

Erica Jong, American poet and writer, 1942-

AUGUST: HAPPINESS

1

Happiness lies in the consciousness

we have of it.

George Sand (Amantine Dupin), French novelist and memoirist, 1804-1876

AUGUST: HAPPINESS

2

Too much of a good thing

can be wonderful.

Mae West, American actor and playwright, 1893-1980

AUGUST: HAPPINESS

3

The greater part of our happiness or misery

depends on our dispositions and

not on our circumstances.

*Martha Washington, the first First Lady of the US,
1731-1802*

AUGUST: HAPPINESS

4

Happiness is not a goal;

it is a by-product.

Eleanor Roosevelt, American humanitarian and First Lady, 1884-1962

AUGUST: HAPPINESS

5

If we only stopped trying to be happy,

we could have a pretty good time.

Edith Wharton. Pulitzer Prize-winning American novelist, and short story writer, 1862-1937

AUGUST: HAPPINESS

6

You're as happy as you allow yourself to be -

so why be unhappy?

Marilyn Quayle, American lawyer, political figure, and novelist, 1949-

AUGUST: HAPPINESS

7

To love what you do and

feel that it matters –

how could anything be more fun?

Katherine Graham, American publisher, 1917-2001

AUGUST: HAPPINESS

8

You've got to S-M-I-L-E

To be H-A-Double-P-Y.

Shirley Temple, American film and television actor and diplomat, 1928-

AUGUST: HAPPINESS

9

That is happiness;

to be dissolved into something complete and great.

Willa Cather, American author, 1873-1947

AUGUST: HAPPINESS

10

They seemed to come

suddenly upon happiness

as if they had surprised

a butterfly in the winter woods.

Edith Wharton. Pulitzer Prize-winning American novelist, and short story writer, 1862-1937

AUGUST: HAPPINESS

11

When one door of happiness closes

another opens;

but often we look so long at the closed door

that we do not see the one

which has been opened for us.

Helen Keller, American lecturer and writer, first deaf blind person to earn a Bachelor of Arts degree, 1880-1968

AUGUST: HAPPINESS

12

Instant gratification takes too long.

Carrie Fisher, American actor, performance artist, and novelist, 1956-

AUGUST: HAPPINESS

13

Happiness is good health and a bad memory.

Ingrid Bergman, Swedish actress, 1915-1962

AUGUST: HAPPINESS

14

When we create something,

we always create it first in a thought form.

If we are basically positive in attitude,

expecting and envisioning pleasure,

satisfaction and happiness,

we will attract and create people,

situations, and events

which conform to our positive expectations.

Shakti Gawain, American author of
Creative Visualization, 1946-

AUGUST: HAPPINESS

15

You will do foolish things,

but do them with enthusiasm.

Colette, French novelist and performer, 1873-1954

AUGUST: HAPPINESS

16

There is joy in self-forgetfulness.

So I try to make

the light in others' eyes my sun,

the music in others' ears my symphony,

the smile on others' lips my happiness.

Helen Keller, American lecturer and writer, first deaf blind person to earn a Bachelor of Arts degree, 1880-1968

AUGUST: HAPPINESS

17

I finally figured out the only reason

to be alive is to enjoy it.

Rita Mae Brown, American writer and feminist, 1944-

AUGUST: HAPPINESS

18

Be happy. It's one way of being wise.

Colette, French novelist and performer, 1873-1954

AUGUST: HAPPINESS

19

Happiness is not a possession to be prized,

it is a quality of thought, a state of mind.

Daphne du Maurier, British author and playwright, 1907-1989

AUGUST: HAPPINESS

20

Your success and happiness lie in you...

Resolve to keep happy,

and your joy and you shall form

an invincible host against difficulties.

Helen Keller, American lecturer and writer, first deaf blind person to earn a Bachelor of Arts degree, 1880-1968

AUGUST: HAPPINESS

21

Don't wait around for other people

to be happy for you.

Any happiness you get

you've got to make yourself.

Alice Walker, American author, poet, and activist, 1944-

AUGUST: HAPPINESS

22

We learn the inner secret of happiness

when we learn to direct our inner drives,

our interest, and our attention

to something outside ourselves.

Ethel Percy Andrus, educator and founder of AARP, 1884-1967

AUGUST: HAPPINESS

23

Happiness must be cultivated. It is like character.

It is not a thing to be safely let alone for a moment,

or it will run to weeds.

Elizabeth Stuart Phelps, American author and early advocate of clothing reform for women, urging them to burn their corsets, 1844-1911

AUGUST: HAPPINESS

24

For with each dawn,

she found new hope that someday,

her dreams of happiness would come true.

Cinderella

AUGUST: HAPPINESS

25

To be kind to all,

to like many and love a few,

to be needed and wanted by those we love,

is certainly the nearest

we can come to happiness.

Mary Stuart, Scottish Queen, 1542-1587

AUGUST: HAPPINESS

26

Whoever is happy

will make others happy too.

Anne Frank, one of the most renowned Jewish victims of the Holocaust, 1929-1945

AUGUST: HAPPINESS

27

I don't think that. . .

one gets a flash of happiness

once and never again;

it is there within you,

and it will come as certainly as death.

Isak Dinesen, Danish author, 1885-1962

AUGUST: HAPPINESS

28

The way to choose happiness

is to follow what is right for you.

Live your own dreams.

And you will know

the meaning of happiness.

Oprah Winfrey, American producer and actor, 1954-

AUGUST: HAPPINESS

29

Just as negative addictions

sneak up on us a day at a time,

so do positive cravings.

Meditation, creative movement,

moments of self-nurturance

that bring contentment

all can become positive habits of wellbeing.

Sarah Ban Breathnach, author of
Simple Abundance

AUGUST: HAPPINESS

30

It is essential to our wellbeing,

and to our lives,

that we play and enjoy life.

Every single day do something

that makes your heart sing.

Marcia Wieder, American author and motivational speaker

AUGUST: HAPPINESS

31

If you obey all the rules,

you miss all the fun.

Katherine Hepburn, American performer, 1907-2003

SEPTEMBER: COURAGE

1

Courage is the price that

life exacts for granting peace.

The soul that knows it not,

knows no release from little things.

Amelia Earhart, noted American aviation pioneer and author, 1897-1937

SEPTEMBER: COURAGE

2

You can't test courage cautiously.

Annie Dillard, American author, 1945-

SEPTEMBER: COURAGE

3

We are not apt to fear for the fearless,

when we are companions in their danger.

George Eliot (Mary Ann Evans), English novelist and journalist, 1819-1880

SEPTEMBER: COURAGE

4

Courage is fear that has said its prayers.

Dorothy Bernard, American screen performer in the silent era, 1890-1955

SEPTEMBER: COURAGE

5

Avoiding danger is no safer in the long run

than outright exposure.

The fearful are caught as often as the bold.

Helen Keller, American lecturer and writer, first deaf blind person to earn a Bachelor of Arts degree, 1880-1968

SEPTEMBER: COURAGE

6

You can't be brave if you've only

had wonderful things happen to you.

Mary Tyler Moore, American
TV sitcom performer, 1936-

SEPTEMBER: COURAGE

7

Life shrinks or expands in proportion

to one's courage.

Anaïs Nin, French-Cuban author, 1903-1977

SEPTEMBER: COURAGE

8

Nothing in life is to be feared.

It is only to be understood.

Marie Curie, Polish physicist and chemist famous for pioneering research on radioactivity, 1867-1934

SEPTEMBER: COURAGE

9

You gain strength, courage, and confidence

by every experience in which you

really stop to look fear in the face . . .

You must do the thing which

you think you cannot do.

Eleanor Roosevelt, American humanitarian and First Lady, 1884-1962

SEPTEMBER: COURAGE

10

Courage is the ladder on which

all the other virtues mount.

Claire Booth Luce, American playwright and US Congresswoman, 1903-1967

SEPTEMBER: COURAGE

11

No coward soul is mine.

Emily Bronte, English novelist and poet, 1818-1846

SEPTEMBER: COURAGE

12

There is plenty of courage among us

for the abstract but not

for the concrete.

Helen Keller, American lecturer and writer, first deaf blind person to earn a Bachelor of Arts degree, 1880-1968

SEPTEMBER: COURAGE

13

The truly fearless think of themselves as normal.

Margaret Atwood, Canadian poet, novelist, and essayist, 1939-

SEPTEMBER: COURAGE

14

It takes far less courage to kill yourself

than it takes to make yourself

wake up one more day.

Judith Rossner, American novelist, 1935-2005

SEPTEMBER: COURAGE

15

Fear is an emotion indispensable for survival.

Hannah Arendt, German American political theorist, 1906-1975

SEPTEMBER: COURAGE

16

Fear is a question:

What are you afraid of, and why?

Our fears are a treasure house of

self-knowledge if we explore them.

Marilyn French, American author and feminist, 1929-2009

SEPTEMBER: COURAGE

17

I wanted you to see what real courage is,

instead of getting the idea that courage

is a man with a gun in his hand.

It's when you know

you're licked before you begin

but you begin anyway and

you see it through no matter what.

Harper Lee, author of
To Kill a Mockingbird, 1926-

SEPTEMBER: COURAGE

18

Always use the proper name for things.

Fear of the name

increases fear of the thing itself.

J. K. Rowling, author of Harry Potter series, 1965-

SEPTEMBER: COURAGE

19

The only courage that matters

is the kind that gets you

from one moment to the next.

Mignon McLaughlin, American journalist and author, 1913-1983

SEPTEMBER: COURAGE

20

The success of life,

the formation of character,

is in proportion to the courage

one has to say to one's own self:

"Thou shalt not."

Carry Nation, radical member of the temperance movement, 1846-1911

SEPTEMBER: COURAGE

21

Courage is like a muscle.

We strengthen it with use.

Ruth Gordon, American performer and writer, 1896-1985

SEPTEMBER: COURAGE

22

Courage can't see around corners

but goes around them anyway.

Mignon McLaughlin, American journalist and author, 1913-1983

SEPTEMBER: COURAGE

23

Everyone thought

I was bold and fearless and even arrogant,

but inside I was always quaking.

Katherine Hepburn, American performer, 1907-2003

SEPTEMBER: COURAGE

24

There are all kinds of courage.

It takes a great deal of bravery

to stand up to our enemies –

but just as much

to stand up to our friends.

J. K. Rowling, author of Harry Potter series, 1965-

SEPTEMBER: COURAGE

25

How cool, how quiet is true courage!

Fanny Burney, English novelist, diarist, and playwright, 1752-1640

SEPTEMBER: COURAGE

26

It is only in his head that

man is heroic;

in the pit of his stomach,

he is always a coward.

Mary Roberts Rinehart, American writer, 1876-1958

SEPTEMBER: COURAGE

27

I think you always feel braver in another language.

Anita Brookner, English novelist and art historian, 1928-

SEPTEMBER: COURAGE

28

Be courageous.

It's one of the only places left uncrowded.

Anita Roddick, founder of The Body Shop,
1942-2007

SEPTEMBER: COURAGE

29

I urge you to be as impudent as you dare.

BE BOLD, BE BOLD, BE BOLD.

Susan Sontag, American essayist and political activist, 1933-2004

SEPTEMBER: COURAGE

30

I'm not afraid of storms,

for I'm learning to sail my ship.

Louisa May Alcott, American novelist and author of Little Women, 1832-1888

OCTOBER: LIFE

1

Life is either a daring adventure or nothing.

To keep our faces toward change and

behave like free spirits in the presence of fate

is strength undefeatable.

Helen Keller, American lecturer and writer, first deaf blind person to earn a Bachelor of Arts degree, 1880-1968

OCTOBER: LIFE

2

Life does not accommodate you, it shatters you.

It is meant to, and it couldn't do it better.

Every seed destroys its container or else

there would be no fruition.

Florida Scott-Maxwell. American playwright and author, 1883-1979

OCTOBER: LIFE

3

Isn't it splendid to think of all the things

there are to find out about?

It just makes me feel glad to be alive –

it's such an interesting world.

It wouldn't be half so interesting

if we knew all about everything, would it?

There'd be no scope for imagination then,

would there?

L. M. Montgomery, Canadian author of
Anne of Green Gables, 1874-1942

OCTOBER: LIFE

4

I am so absorbed in the wonder

of earth and the life upon it that

I cannot think of heaven and the angels.

I have enough for this life.

Pearl S. Buck, American writer, 1892-1973

OCTOBER: LIFE

5

Life itself is the proper binge.

Julia Child, American chef, author, and TV personality, 1912-2004

OCTOBER: LIFE

6

It has begun to occur to me

that life is a stage

I'm going through.

Ellen Goodman, American journalist and Pulitzer Prize-winning syndicated columnist, 1941-

OCTOBER: LIFE

7

Life is something to do

when you can't get to sleep.

Fran Lebowitz, American humorist and social commentator, 1950-

OCTOBER: LIFE

8

Life is a frail moth flying

Caught in the web of the years that pass.

Sara Teasdale, American lyrical poet, 1884-1933

OCTOBER: LIFE

9

Life is like a great jazz riff.

You sense the end the very moment

you were wanting it to go on forever.

Sheila Ballantyne, American writer

OCTOBER: LIFE

10

Life is better than death, I believe,

if only because it is less boring,

and because it has fresh peaches in it.

Alice Walker, American author, poet, and activist, 1944-

OCTOBER: LIFE

11

Life offstage has sometimes been

a wilderness of unpredictables

in an unchoreographed world.

Margot Fonteyn, one of the greatest classical ballet dancers of all time, 1919-1991

OCTOBER: LIFE

12

What you get is a living –

what you give is a life.

Lillian Gish, American stage screen, and television performer, 1893-1993

OCTOBER: LIFE

13

I began to have an idea of my life,

not as the slow shaping of achievements

to fit my preconceived purposes,

but as the gradual discovery and

growth of a purpose which I did not know.

Joanna Field (Marion Milner), British author and psychoanalyst, 1900-1998

OCTOBER: LIFE

14

All [life] is a pattern . . .

but we can't always see the pattern

when we're part of it.

Belva Plain, American author of mainstream fiction, 1915-2010

OCTOBER: LIFE

15

I don't want to get to the end of my life and

find that I lived just the length of it.

I want to have lived the width of it as well.

Diane Ackerman, American author, poet, and naturalist, 1948-

OCTOBER: LIFE

16

Life isn't a matter of milestones but of moments.

Rose Kennedy, American philanthropist, 1890-1995

OCTOBER: LIFE

17

Life is easier than you'd think:

all that is necessary is

to accept the impossible,

do without the indispensable,

and bear the intolerable.

Kathleen Norris, American novelist, 1880-1966

OCTOBER: LIFE

18

Life is the only real counselor;

wisdom unfiltered

through personal experience

does not become

a part of the moral tissue.

Edith Wharton. Pulitzer Prize-winning American novelist, and short story writer, 1862-1937

OCTOBER: LIFE

19

You make what seems a simple choice:

choose a man or a job or a neighborhood –

and what you have chosen is

not a man or a job or a neighborhood,

but a life.

Jessamyn West, American writer, 1902-1964

OCTOBER: LIFE

20

How we spend our days is, of course,

how we spend our lives.

Annie Dillard, American author, 1945-

OCTOBER: LIFE

21

I have not loved enough.

I'd been busy, busy, so busy,

preparing for life,

while life floated by me,

quiet, and swift as a regatta.

Lorene Cary, American author, educator, and social activist, 1956-

OCTOBER: LIFE

22

You know, your career is just your career.

Your life is your *life*!

Sissy Spacek, American performer and singer, 1949-

OCTOBER: LIFE

23

I like living.

I have sometimes been

wildly, despairingly, acutely miserable,

racked with sorrow, but through it all

I still know quite certainly

that just to *be alive* is a grand thing.

Agatha Christie, British crime writer, 1890-1976

OCTOBER: LIFE

24

Life was meant to be lived,

and curiosity must be kept alive.

One must never, for whatever reason,

turn his back on life.

Eleanor Roosevelt, American humanitarian and First Lady, 1884-1962

OCTOBER: LIFE

25

Life forms illogical patterns.

It is haphazard and full of beauties

which I try to catch as they fly by,

for who knows whether

any of them will ever return?

Margot Fonteyn, one of the greatest classical ballet dancers of all time, 1919-1991

OCTOBER: LIFE

26

Life is what we make it,

always has been, always will be.

Grandma Moses, renowned American folk artist, 1860-1961

OCTOBER: LIFE

27

Not everyone's life is what they make it.

Some people's life is

what other people make it.

Alice Walker, American author, poet, and activist, 1944-

OCTOBER: LIFE

28

Men for the sake of getting a living

forget to live.

Margaret Fuller, American journalist and women's rights advocate, 1810-1850

OCTOBER: LIFE

29

Many people live and die with

their music still unplayed.

They never dare to try.

Mary Kay Ash, founder of Mary Kay Cosmetics, 1918-2001

OCTOBER: LIFE

30

Mistakes are the dues one pays for a full life.

Sophia Loren, Italian actress, 1934-

OCTOBER: LIFE

31

The bread of life is love,

the salt of life is work,

the sweetness of life is poesy,

and the water of life is faith.

Anna Jameson, British writer, 1794-1860

NOVEMBER: GRATITUDE

1

When you come right down to it,

the secret of having it all

is loving it all.

Joyce Brothers, American psychologist and advice columnist, 1927-

NOVEMBER: GRATITUDE

2

I have come to understand that

every day is something to cherish.

Kerri Strug, American gymnast, 1977-

NOVEMBER: GRATITUDE

3

One can never pay in gratitude;

one can only pay "in kind"

somewhere else in life.

Anne Morrow Lindbergh, American nonfiction writer and poet, 1906-2001

NOVEMBER: GRATITUDE

4

Gratitude is an opener of locked-up blessings.

Marianne Williamson, American spiritual activist, author, and founder of The Peace Alliance, 1953-

NOVEMBER: GRATITUDE

5

When I surrendered my desire for
security and sought serenity instead,
I looked at my life with open eyes.
I saw that I had much for which to be grateful.
I felt humbled by my riches and regretted that
I took for granted the abundance that
already existed in my life.
How could I expect more from the universe
when I didn't appreciate
what I already had?

Sarah Ban Breathnach, author of
Simple Abundance

NOVEMBER: GRATITUDE

6

Today I offer a prayer of forgiveness:

forgive the pettiness of my ingratitude...

the absence of profound thankfulness.

Mary Anne Radmacher, American author and artist

NOVEMBER: GRATITUDE

7

Learn everything you can,

anytime you can, from anyone you can –

there will always come a time when

you will be grateful you did.

Sarah Caldwell, American opera conductor, impresario, and stage director of opera, 1924-2006

NOVEMBER: GRATITUDE

8

I move through my day-to-day life with a
sense of appreciation and gratitude that
comes from knowing how
fortunate I truly am and how unearned
all that I am thankful for really is.
Every time I see beauty around me
I appreciate what I am seeing, and
simultaneously I have this sense of appreciation -
for being alive to have this particular moment.

Jean Shinoda Bolen, American psychiatrist, activist, and author

NOVEMBER: GRATITUDE

9

When something does not

insist on being noticed,

when we aren't grabbed by the collar

or struck on the skull

by a presence or an event,

we take for granted the very things that

most deserve our gratitude.

Cynthia Ozick, American-Jewish short story writer, novelist, and essayist, 1928-

NOVEMBER: GRATITUDE

10

Gratitude helps you grow and expand;

gratitude brings joy and laughter

into your life and into the lives

of those around you.

Eileen Caddy, New Age author and spiritual teacher, 1917-2006

NOVEMBER: GRATITUDE

11

When you cultivate gratitude,

you become a happier,

more fulfilled person.

The more you're grateful for,

the more blessings will come to you.

Susan Santucci, Pathways to the Spirit, 1999

NOVEMBER: GRATITUDE

12

Instead of comparing our lot with that

of those who are more fortunate than we are,

we should compare it with the lot

of the great majority of our fellow men.

It then appears that

we are among the privileged.

Helen Keller, American lecturer and writer, first deaf blind person to earn a Bachelor of Arts degree, 1880-1968

NOVEMBER: GRATITUDE

13

Whatever our individual

troubles and challenges may be,

it's important to pause every now and then to

appreciate all that we have, on every level.

We need to literally "count our blessings,"

give thanks for them,

allow ourselves to enjoy them, and

relish the experience of prosperity

we already have.

Shakti Gawain, American author of
Creative Visualization, 1946-

NOVEMBER: GRATITUDE

14

Real life isn't always going to

be perfect or go our way,

but the recurring acknowledgement of

what is working in our lives

can help us not only to survive

but surmount our difficulties.

Sarah Ban Breathnach, author of
Simple Abundance

NOVEMBER: GRATITUDE

15

Part of the journey toward joy involves

not waiting around for trouble,

but being continuously aware

of our blessings.

Charlotte Davis Kasl, American psychologist and author

NOVEMBER: GRATITUDE

16

Blessed are those

who can give without remembering,

and take without forgetting.

Elizabeth Bibesco, English writer, 1897-1945

NOVEMBER: GRATITUDE

17

In the end, though,

maybe we must all give up trying

to pay back the people in this world

who sustain our lives.

In the end, maybe it's wiser to surrender before

the miraculous scope of human generosity

and to just keep saying

thank you, forever and sincerely,

for as long as we have voices.

Elizabeth Gilbert, author of
Eat, Pray, Love, 1969-

NOVEMBER: GRATITUDE

18

Glee! The great storm is over!

Emily Dickinson, American poet, 1830-1886

NOVEMBER: GRATITUDE

19

Appreciation is yeast,

lifting ordinary to extraordinary.

Mary-Ann Petro

NOVEMBER: GRATITUDE

20

Our indebtedness . . . is not virtue;

our repayment is.

Virtue begins when

we dedicate ourselves

actively to the job of gratitude.

Ruth Benedict, American anthropologist and folklorist, 1887-1948

NOVEMBER: GRATITUDE

21

It may be more blessed

to give than to receive,

but there is more grace

in receiving than giving.

When you receive,

whom do you love and praise?

The giver.

When you give, the same holds true.

Jessamyn West, American writer, 1902-1964

NOVEMBER: GRATITUDE

22

The more you praise and

celebrate your life,

the more there is in life

to celebrate.

Oprah Winfrey, American producer and actor, 1954-

NOVEMBER: GRATITUDE

23

Silent gratitude isn't

very much to anyone.

Gertrude Stein, American writer and playwright, 1874-1946

NOVEMBER: GRATITUDE

24

Gratitude unlocks the fullness of life.

It turns what we have into enough,

and more. It turns denial into acceptance,

chaos to order, confusion to clarity.

It can turn a meal into a feast,

a house into a home,

a stranger into a friend.

Gratitude makes sense of our past,

brings peace for today, and

creates a vision for tomorrow.

Melody Beattie, author of
Codependent No More, 1987

NOVEMBER: GRATITUDE

25

Remember that not to be happy

is not to be grateful.

Elizabeth Carter, English poet, classicist, and writer, 1717-1806

NOVEMBER: GRATITUDE

26

So often we dwell on the things that

seem impossible rather than on

the things that are possible.

So often we are depressed

by what remains to be done and

forget to be thankful

for all that has been done.

Marian Wright Edelman, American activist for children's rights, 1939-

NOVEMBER: GRATITUDE

27

Joy is a heart full and a mind

purified by gratitude.

Marietta McCarthy, American author

NOVEMBER: GRATITUDE

28

Gratitude is riches.

Complaint is poverty.

Doris Day, American performer and singer, 1924-

NOVEMBER: GRATITUDE

29

Grace isn't a little prayer you chant

before receiving a meal.

It's a way of life.

Jacqueline Winspear, writer of popular
Maisie Dobbs mystery series

NOVEMBER: GRATITUDE

30

What you focus on expands,

and when you focus on

the goodness in your life,

you create more of it.

Opportunities, relationships, even money

flowed my way when

I learned to be grateful

no matter what happened in my life.

Oprah Winfrey, American producer
and actor, 1954-

NOVEMBER: GRATITUDE

31

Appreciation can make a day,

even change a life.

Your willingness to put it into words

is all that is necessary.

Margaret Cousins

DECEMBER: PRINCIPLES AND TRUTHS

1

The first problem for all of us,

men and women,

is not to learn,

but to unlearn.

Gloria Steinem, American feminist, journalist, and social and political activist, 1934-

DECEMBER: PRINCIPLES AND TRUTHS

2

There are no dangerous thoughts;

thinking itself is dangerous.

Hannah Arendt, German American political theorist, 1906-1975

DECEMBER: PRINCIPLES AND TRUTHS

3

It is worse than folly . . .

not to recognize the truth,

for in it lies the tinder for tomorrow.

Pearl S. Buck, American writer, 1892-1973

DECEMBER: PRINCIPLES AND TRUTHS

4

I do not want the peace

which passeth understanding;

I want the understanding

which bringeth peace.

Helen Keller, American lecturer and writer, first deaf blind person to earn a Bachelor of Arts degree, 1880-1968

DECEMBER: PRINCIPLES AND TRUTHS

5

I have a simple philosophy.

Fill what's empty. Empty what's full.

And scratch what itches.

Alice Roosevelt Longworth, American wit and society leader, 1884-1980

DECEMBER: PRINCIPLES AND TRUTHS

6

Learn to get in touch with silence

within yourself and know that

everything in this life has a purpose.

There are no mistakes, no coincidences,

all events are blessings

given to us to learn from.

Elisabeth Kubler Ross, Swiss American psychiatrist, author, and pioneer in Near-death studies, 1926-2004

DECEMBER: PRINCIPLES AND TRUTHS

7

We cannot take anything for granted

beyond the first mathematical formulae.

Question everything else.

Maria Mitchell, first American woman to work as a professional astronomer, 1818-1889

DECEMBER: PRINCIPLES AND TRUTHS

8

The dedicated life is

the life worth living.

You must give

with your whole heart.

Annie Dillard, American author, 1945-

DECEMBER: PRINCIPLES AND TRUTHS

9

A soul occupied with great ideas

best performs small duties.

Harriet Martineau, English social theorist, often cited as the first female sociologist, 1802-1876

DECEMBER: PRINCIPLES AND TRUTHS

10

Study as if you are going to live forever;

live as if you are going to die tomorrow.

Marion Mitchell, New Zealand singer, 1876-1955

DECEMBER: PRINCIPLES AND TRUTHS

11

The truth is friendship is every bit

as sacred and eternal as marriage.

Katherine Mansfield, New Zealand-born modernist writer of short fiction, 1888-1923

DECEMBER: PRINCIPLES AND TRUTHS

12

Truth is like heat or light;

its vibrations are endless

and are endlessly felt.

Margaret Deland, American novelist, 1857-1945

DECEMBER: PRINCIPLES AND TRUTHS

13

The way I see it,

if you want the rainbow,

you gotta put up with the rain.

Dolly Parton, American singer-songwriter, 1946-

DECEMBER: PRINCIPLES AND TRUTHS

14

While others may argue about whether

the world ends with a bang or a whimper,

I just want to make sure

mine doesn't end with a whine.

Barbara Gordon, American writer

DECEMBER: PRINCIPLES AND TRUTHS

15

Sanity is a cozy lie.

Susan Sontag, American essayist and political activist, 1933-2004

DECEMBER: PRINCIPLES AND TRUTHS

16

Art is not a study of positive reality;

it is the seeking for ideal truth.

George Sand (Amantine Dupin), French novelist and memoirist, 1804-1876

DECEMBER: PRINCIPLES AND TRUTHS

17

Some truths are moral illnesses.

Marilyn French, American author and feminist, 1929-2009

DECEMBER: PRINCIPLES AND TRUTHS

18

I can therefore I am.

Simone Weil, French philosopher and social activist, 1909-1943

DECEMBER: PRINCIPLES AND TRUTHS

19

The only causes of regret are

laziness, outbursts of temper,

hurting others, prejudice,

jealousy, and envy.

Germaine Greer, Australian writer and scholar, 1939-

DECEMBER: PRINCIPLES AND TRUTHS

20

It is a wholesome and necessary thing for us

to turn again to the earth and

in the contemplation of her beauties

to know the sense of wonder and humility.

Rachel Carson, American marine biologist and conservationist, 1907-1964

DECEMBER: PRINCIPLES AND TRUTHS

21

Suffering is also one of the ways

of knowing you're alive.

Jessamyn West, American writer, 1902-1964

DECEMBER: PRINCIPLES AND TRUTHS

22

One cannot think well,

love, well, sleep well –

if one has not dined well.

Virginia Woolf, English author, essayist, and publisher, 1882-1941

DECEMBER: PRINCIPLES AND TRUTHS

23

Do not do what you

would undo if caught.

Leah Arendt

DECEMBER: PRINCIPLES AND TRUTHS

24

I have come to the conclusion,

after many years of

sometimes sad experience,

that you cannot come

to any conclusions at all.

Vita Sackville-West, English author and poet, 1892-1962

DECEMBER: PRINCIPLES AND TRUTHS

25

Make no judgments

where you have no compassion.

Anne McCaffrey, American-born Irish writer, 1926-2011

DECEMBER: PRINCIPLES AND TRUTHS

26

Is it really so difficult to tell

a good action from a bad one?

I think one usually knows right away

or a moment afterward,

in a horrid flash of regret.

Mary *McCarthy, American novelist, critic, and memoirist, 1912-1989*

DECEMBER: PRINCIPLES AND TRUTHS

27

We are human beings trying to be spiritual.

We are spiritual beings trying to be human.

Jacquelyn Small, American writer on spiritual psychology

DECEMBER: PRINCIPLES AND TRUTHS

28

Spirituality leaps where

science cannot yet follow, because science

must always test and measure,

and much of reality and human experience

is immeasurable.

Starhawk, American writer and activist, 1951-

DECEMBER: PRINCIPLES AND TRUTHS

29

Vitality!

That's the pursuit of life, isn't it?

Katherine Hepburn, American performer, 1907-2003

DECEMBER: PRINCIPLES AND TRUTHS

30

Whenever two good people

argue over principles,

they are both right.

Maria von Ebner-Eschenbach, Austrian writer, 1830-1916

DECEMBER: PRINCIPLES AND TRUTHS

31

Never worry too much about

the things you can replace;

worry only about

the things you can't replace.

Winnie Johnson

ABOUT THE AUTHOR

Georgiana Carollus, spiritual and life coach (www.coachingwithspirit.com) and career services professional (www.resumeswithspirit.com), is passionate about helping others identify and embrace their uniqueness and strengths. She has a keen interest in creativity, intuition, and incorporating spiritual values into daily life and work..

Contact Georgiana for information about her services at gc@coachingwithspirit.com.

Printed in Great Britain
by Amazon

58346590R00209